The Caste War of Yucatán: The History and Legacy of the Last Major Indigenous Revolt in the Americas

By Charles River Editors

A contemporary painting of the Caste War

Charles River Editors is a boutique digital publishing company, specializing in bringing history back to life with educational and engaging books on a wide range of topics. Keep up to date with our new and free offerings with this 5 second sign up on our weekly mailing list, and visit Our Kindle Author Page to see other recently published Kindle titles.

We make these books for you and always want to know our readers' opinions, so we encourage you to leave reviews and look forward to publishing new and exciting titles each week.

Introduction

A model map of the peninsula with Mayan settlements marked across it

"Beneath the peninsula's tranquil surface there has always existed a deep current of conflict." - Douglas W. Richmond

The Yucatán Peninsula, one of the few in the world to project northward, was already a land of extraordinary events since prehistoric times. Considered today as a place of exceptional beauty, it was described as "a very sad country" by the first Spanish chroniclers. Full of very flat land without mountains, hard soil, extreme weather and scant vegetation, it was the cradle of one of the earliest civilizations and perhaps the most advanced one in the Western Hemisphere: the Maya.

Of all the world's civilizations, few have intrigued people more than the Maya, whose culture, astronomy, language, and mysterious disappearance all continue to captivate people. In 2012 especially, there has been a renewed focus on the Mayans, whose advanced calendar has led many to speculate the world will end on the same date the Mayan calendar ends. The focus on the "doomsday" scenario, however, has overshadowed the Mayans' true contribution to astronomy, language, sports, and art.

When the Spaniards "discovered" Yucatán, they thought it was an island. Although they later realized that it was part of the vast country that Cortés had conquered, they were not very wrong to think of it as an isle, considering the zealous and independent spirit that has characterized its inhabitants then and now. Although it has been part of Mexico for 170 years, it was encouraged by the example of Texas, compelling the peninsula to twice proclaim its independence and create the short-lived Republic of Yucatán. Many presidents in Mexico had to repress the great peninsula that, despite its longing for independence, had a vibrant foreign trade with the world capitals and a privileged geographical location, even as it lacked the abundance of resources that Texas and California possessed.

It was especially the cultivation of henequen, a resistant fiber obtained from an agave that's useful for many industries, that propelled the economic development in Yucatán. This helped interest many capitalists when it came to settling in Mérida, one of the most beautiful cities in Mexico and the Americas, the so-called "white city."

As that suggests, Yucatán was not a wasteland when the first shipwrecked, battered Spaniards arrived on its shores. In fact, they found the descendants of an ancient civilization who refused to be conquered and who, when they finally succumbed to the steel and germs of the Europeans, refused to assimilate and instead disappeared into the jungle. By the mid-19th century, virtually all the native peoples of America had been defeated or were fleeing in small bands from canyon to canyon, only for the Maya to lead the last great, indigenous rebellion in the Yucatán, attempting to shake off the white domain initiated through the conquest of Spain. The so-called "Caste War" was a total war, much larger than the skirmishes with the Native Americans in the United States around the same time. While the Apaches and Comanches were barely bands of men attacking towns and ranches, wandering homeless, the Mayan rebellion was nothing less than a war of annihilation in an attempt to take back their former nation.

For many years, large portions of the peninsula were under the control of these proud Native Americans, leaving its roads and jungles essentially forbidden to the white man. Ironically, these events would help Western academics "rediscover" the Maya civilization, and several archaeological and scientific expeditions began to dig up the cities, monuments, and pyramids that make this part of Mexico one of the most frequented places by international tourists today. Thus, while a successful hotel industry was growing in the "very sad country" with the most spectacular beaches, and the ancient Mayan cities were acclaimed, their descendants were left in poverty and oblivion.

Using the weapons that they retained from service in the Yucatec army and weapons supplied by the British through Belize, the Mayan insurgents in the Caste War, as it came to be known, almost succeeded in taking over the entire Yucatan. However, on the eve of what would have been a successful siege of Mérida, the Maya soldiers gave up and returned to their fields. Pursued by the Yucatec forces, the Maya melted back into the jungle and formed communities that exist to this day.

The Caste War of Yucatán: The History and Legacy of the Last Major Indigenous Revolt in the Americas examines the events that brought about the rebellion, the people who fought it, and the results. Along with pictures and a bibliography, you will learn about the Caste War like never before.

The Yucatán and the Maya

The Yucatán is located at the eastern end of the Mexican Republic, and the region has played a vital role in the history of the world, all the way back to tens of millions of years ago. In many ways, the planet as it exists today came about because of a natural disaster that occurred 66 million years ago in the vicinity of the modern town of Chicxulub, on the north coast of the Yucatán Peninsula, where a meteorite or comet seven to 50 miles long hit the planet with a magnitude of 100 million megatons, more potent than a billion bombs like the nuclear weapon used on Hiroshima. The meteorite formed a crater 60 miles long and 20 miles deep, and its remains are still visible at the bottom of the Caribbean Sea. Scientists estimate that the impact force was so enormous that some of the rocks expelled landed on the Moon, while other fragments entered Earth's orbit and continued to travel through space. The largest and heaviest chunks returned with destructive force to the ground in minutes. The impact caused volcanic eruptions, gigantic tsunamis, burned the forests, and acidified the oceans, extinguishing most of the planet's life. The date coincides with the mass extinction of dinosaurs, and further analysis of the data indicates that the Chicxulub meteor and the mass extinction of gigantic reptiles are related. The Yucatán meteor, a catastrophic day for all life on the planet, marked the first day of the Cenozoic Era.

At that time, Yucatán was underwater, but 40 million years after the impact, the land slowly emerged from the ocean. Geologically, the peninsula is a flat land, with slight protrusions and hollows. Since the soil and subsoil are very permeable and rainwater infiltrates rapidly and feeds the phreatic deposits, Yucatán has no rivers, with the exception of Champotón, which is short. The soil is hard and calcareous, so agriculture is difficult, and the rains are scarce and erratic. Groundwater moves slowly and flows into the sea, away from the coast. These underground currents dissolve the limestone of the soil and form cavities with water at the bottom. In some cases they have small mouths that extend inwards, and sometimes, when the entire roof of the cave collapses, a large mirror of water can be seen at the bottom, between vertical or low-slope rocky walls. These are the so-called cenotes, and these natural wonders have had a great influence in the life of the region. Considered as sacred places by the Mayans, the cenotes of clear waters and underground caverns connecting each other allowed people to flourish in Yucatán at a time when philosophy was being refined in ancient Greece. The Maya reached their peak around the time Emperor Constantine decreed freedom of religious cults across the Roman Empire.

Jaguars, pumas and other wild cats live in the mountains south of the peninsula, and deer, pigs, monkeys and other mammals also call the region home. There are snakes and lizards, and among the birds are pheasants, turkeys, macaws, parrots, and toucans. There are countless insects, with bees being the most abundant.

Today the Aztecs are remembered as the civilization with the vast empire, but the Mayans spread across a wide swath of land themselves. The region of Mesoamerica inhabited by the Maya stretched from the dry, flat limestone plains of the Yucatan to the wet, mountainous jungle of Chiapas and Guatemala and on to the narrow flatland of the Pacific coast. The first inhabitants of the region are believed to have been hunter gatherers, and anthropologists think these primitive people were descended from the early migrants who moved from Asia across to the northern reaches of North America and spread south around 14000 BCE Once settled, a more agricultural society developed in central Mexico in the fifth millennium BCE. These people were able to reliably grow crops of corn, beans and squashes through slash and burn field preparation, but depending on the quantity and quality of the soil, a field had a limited life expectancy. In some regions, particularly those where the soil cover was thin and the rainfall limited, the slash and burn technique of crop cultivation required careful attention to the seasonal weather pattern.

Around 1800 BCE, the Olmecs, the earliest traceable civilization of Mesoamerica, built cities that depended on reliable agricultural production. Many details of Olmec society remain a mystery, but it is known that some of their practices, such as building pyramids and playing a ritual ball game, were similar to those of the later Maya. Nevertheless, the precise relationship between the Olmec and the Maya culture is as yet unknown. What is known is that while the earliest Maya communities on the Pacific coast and in the Guatemalan highlands and Belize were on the rise, the Olmec civilization, with its population centers near the region of modern Veracruz and Villahermosa in Mexico, was in decline.

The history of the Maya is divided into periods that have been given names and dates that are not currently unanimously accepted. The nomenclature of the chronology of Maya civilization was created by Eurocentric scholars who held fixed ideas on the rise, flourishing and decline of civilizations, in keeping with the tracking of the Greek and Roman empires of antiquity. In particular, readers should be cautious of the word classic, as it implies a superior rank or model or standard which does not really apply to the evolution of Maya culture. Still, this chronology, even with its imperfections, does allow for a quick survey of the evolution of Maya civilization.

The Early Preclassic period dating from 1800-900 BCE is the era when the Olmecs established their major cities at Paso de la Amada in Chiapas and San Lorenzo in southern Veracruz. In the Middle Preclassic Period, spanning the years from 900 to 300 BCE, the first Maya cities were built on the Pacific coast, in places like Itzapa near Tapachula, in the Guatemalan highlands at such sites as Kaminaljuyú now underneath Guatemala City, and the recently excavated mega-city El Mirador. It is currently held that Maya city building expanded north further into the Guatemalan Highlands and Belize.

It was in the Late Preclassic Period from 300 BCE-250 CE that archaeologists believe Maya culture developed a high level of complexity. This included the appearance of writing in the Mayan language and a sophisticated continuing calendar system. In the Early Classic Period, 250-600 CE, Maya civilization flourished, particularly in the city of Tikal in modern Guatemala.

Major construction was carried out at Copán in modern Honduras and at Palenque in Chiapas, Mexico. The Late Classic, 600-950 CE, is used by historians to designate the age in which civilization reached its height. This was the time when the great cities of the Yucatan or northern lowlands flourished and the cities of the southern lowlands declined. It was also late in this period that the city of Chichen Itza rose to prominence.

The Main Plaza at Tikal

The final period in the chronology used by scholars of Maya civilization is the Post Classic Period, 950-1530 CE, which saw the collapse of Chichen Itza and the rise of Mayapán, the last leading city of Maya culture. The four surviving Mayan codices were written during this period.

Given the manner in which Maya cities flourished in different periods and were built in different environments, from the lush jungle in the south to the wet coastlands of Belize and the dry limestone plains of the Yucatan, it is not surprising that the Maya were not a homogenous people. In different regions of their empire, Mayan people and cities had distinctly different economies, social organization, art and architecture. Variation existed over time and geography. It is important to keep that in mind when discussing Mayan culture.

In general, the society of the Maya was stratified. The king who owed his position to a royal lineage was surrounded by nobles that obtained their rank through paternal descent, although their status was even higher if they were also descended from nobility on the maternal side. Among the nobility in some Maya cities were prosperous farmers, successful merchants, priests and warriors. The duties of the court included maintaining civic order, recording the history of the community in sculpture and inscriptions, keeping the calendar, recording astronomical information and divining the future from it, and managing war and trade. Below the nobility were the free workers who were allocated a *hun* or *uinic* of 400 square feet of land to farm. They paid an in-kind levy to the king and temple priests, who would divine ideal times for planting and harvest. The Mayans strongly that neither good things nor bad things occurred by chance, which is why they were so bent on studying the patterns of the sun and stars. They believed these patterns were set in motion by the gods to help the Maya reveal their divine intentions.

The vast majority of the population of Maya cities consisted of farmers, who mostly lived in wood-framed reed huts on an elevated platform, much like those that can be seen today in rural Mayan communities in the Yucatan. This was sensible, since a high level of food production was necessary to sustain populations that were quite astonishing in size. In the Late Classic period around 600 CE, the city of Tikal in Guatemala is estimated to have had a population of 39,000 people, with another 10,000 living in the hinterland around the city. At its peak, Palenque had about 6,000 inhabitants, Uxmal had perhaps 15,000, and Chichen Itza may have had over 30,000 inhabitants. With different features and climates, the methods and successes of farming around these various communities were not always similar. In the northern lowlands, cities such as Uxmal and Chichen Itza had precarious food supplies that depended, in part, on slash and burn agriculture. In the farthest reaches of the southern lowlands, at cities like Palenque, water was plentiful and reliable crop production was the norm. Here, because the depth of the soil was significantly more than that of the northern lowlands, cleared land could be productive for 10 years or longer.

Depending on the location of their community, the Mayans typically ate animals that they hunted, and along the shore in the Yucatan at maritime trading cities like Cozumel and Tulum, and in Belize, the Maya had a diet that included quantities of fish.

While it has historically been the Aztecs who were viewed as a militaristic civilization, there is considerable debate among scholars on the question of territorial aggression among the Maya. Because many of the Maya cities lack fortifications that are like those Eurocentric archaeologists might have expected, it was once assumed that the Maya created for themselves an ideal, pacifistic society. But others have considered the Maya as particularly ferocious in warfare, taking captives for ritual sacrifice and appropriating territories through force. Still others have explained the demise of certain Maya cities by arguing that they were devastated by internecine warfare that doomed both sides of the fighting. As with many aspects of Maya society, the presence or absence of bellicose behavior is an enigma. There have been some findings of parapets and ramparts, in particular at Tikal and Becán, clear proof that the Mayans saw the need for defensive fortifications for those cities. But the fact that such ramparts were not a consistent part of Maya city construction is evidence that there was considerable variation in aggression, expansion and cooperation from one city to another.

Eventually the great Maya cities began to lose their populations, one by one. The collapse came first to the cities of the southern lowlands. For example, building came to a halt and ritual ceremonies were abandoned at Palenque in 799 and Tikal in 879. In the northern lowlands of the Yucatan, the cities of the Puuc hills such as Uxmal were abandoned starting around 920, and Chichen Itza was partially abandoned in 948. The culture of the Maya survived in a disorganized way until it was revived at Mayapán around 1200.

Why Maya cities were abandoned and left to be overgrown by the jungle is a puzzle that intrigues curious people around the world today, especially those who have a penchant for speculating on lost civilizations. Often, conjecture on the cause of the end of the Maya civilization has depended on the preconceptions of the observer. If one were to ask Spanish Bishop Landa why the Maya he met and talked to were in such a sorry state, he would have said that their condition was a result of their unbaptized state. Some American archaeologists, living in the era of frighteningly bloody mass wars of the 20th century, suggested that the Maya destroyed themselves by constant civil warfare. Others writing in the era of the rise of Communism believed that Maya cities collapsed because of class warfare. In the 21st century, a more common theory on the collapse of the Maya is that they were forced by drought, overpopulation, and unsustainable agricultural practices to move away from their urban centers. What probably happened was that some or all of these social and environmental factors converged in such a way that even the strongest of Maya cities were unable to survive.

The Arrival of Europeans

When the first European ships arrived on the peninsula, which they mistook for an island, the Mayan civilization was in full decline. The ceremonial centers were abandoned, the great monuments were buried under a green layer of vegetation, and only small communities persisted, scattered in the jungle. Chichen Itza, the great city of the empire in central Yucatán, was still visited as a sacred place, but the Spaniards, not suspecting that they were stepping on the cradle of one of the five great civilizations of antiquity, found only a handful of independent states, which they called provinces.

Before the first major expedition was organized, a small party of Europeans arrived in Yucatán, a dozen Spaniards who had sailed from Panama to Santo Domingo and shipwrecked in the Sea of the Antilles in 1511. They drifted for several days until they reached some unknown white sand beaches, and when they entered the strange country, they were attacked by their inhabitants. At least two of them survived, a sailor named Jerónimo de Aguilar and another named Gonzalo Guerrero.

In 1517 Francisco Hernández de Córdoba arrived at the island of Cozumel and headed to present-day Campeche, but he was attacked by the rebellious settlers and went back to Cuba, where he gave notice to Spain of the discovery of what he thought was an island. Two years later, Hernán Cortés, destined to meet the Aztec's Emperor Montezuma in central Mexico, left

Cuba and arrived in Cozumel, where he learned that there were a few Spanish sailors shipwrecked in Yucatán. Thus, he set out to rescue them.

Cortés

When Cortés found Jerónimo de Aguilar, he did not recognize him - after eight years, Aguilar was no longer fluent in Spanish, he was dressed as a native, and he had tanned skin. Since he had also learned the language of the Mayans, Cortés figured that would be of great advantage for him and his conquistadores, so he began using Aguilar as an interpreter.

After Aguilar was "rescued," the party searched for his shipwrecked mate, Gonzalo Guerrero, who lived in another town. Ultimately, however, Guerrero refused to leave with Cortés, and his words were kept in the annals thanks to contemporary writer Bernal Díaz del Castillo: "Brother, I am married and have three children. Go with God, I have my face carved and my eyebrows pierced (referring to the ornaments in the Mayan style that he was wearing). And you see these, my little children, how beautiful they are."

Guerrero was so appreciated in his village that he had been made a captain in times of war. He was also likely the father of the first mixed race Mexican of European and indigenous descent. Aguilar tried to convince his partner to join, and he assured Guerrero that if he wanted, he could bring his children. Guerrero's wife, a Mayan woman, confronted Aguilar and told him to leave and never return. In the end, Guerrero lived among the Maya until the end of his life, dying while fighting the Spanish in defense of his adopted people.

As Cortés destroyed the Aztec Empire, the Yucatán was mostly not subjected to the Spanish Conquest, but near the end of 1526, Spain's King Charles I granted permission to Francisco de Montejo, who had participated in the conquest of Tenochtitlan, to lead an expedition into the peninsula. The first attempt failed due to illness and shortage of supplies, and in less than a year Montejo, who tried to found the first city among the ruins of Chichen Itza, had to terminate his enterprise.

Montejo came back three years later better prepared, and the conquest of the peninsula was especially cruel. The Spaniards burned alive many of the principal men among the Maya, set fire to the villages, hung women from the trees, and hung their children from their mothers' feet. Diego de Landa described the depredations: "They cut off noses, arms and legs, and threw the women out in deep lagoons with pumpkins tied to their feet; they beat the children if they did not walk as fast as the mothers, and if they became ill, or did not walk as much as the others, they cut off their heads."[1]

The Yucatán was set to have its encounter with Christianity, and it would be an extremely violent one. Back in Spain, Diego de Landa, the second Spanish bishop of the Roman Catholic Archdiocese of Yucatán, wrote a list or "relations" of all the things he saw in the land. He mentioned, for example, how people lived for many years, and that he had found a 104-year-old man among the natives. He also wrote that the buildings on the peninsula were the most notable of what had been discovered thus far on the continent, and that shortly before the conquest, the region had been swept away by different calamities, including hurricanes, plagues, and wars. De Landa was interested in forging links with the inhabitants and learning everything he could from them, including their language, manuscripts, and history, but only so that he could more thoroughly destroy the culture and documents. As a result, the bishop was responsible for the destruction of many codices and hundreds of pieces of art. He wrote, "We found a large number of books and, since they contained nothing but superstitions and lies of the devil, we burned them all, which they lamented to an amazing degree and caused them great distress." When the bishop found several skulls in a cave, he escalated the tortures to obtain forced confessions and get the natives to admit that they still practiced human sacrifice.

---

[1] Diego de Landa, *Relación de las cosas de Yucatán.*

De Landa

The Franciscan priest enforced the Inquisition with such cruelty on men and women because they knew nothing about Christianity, and for this reason he called them diabolic. He would go down in history as one of the most intolerant and bloodthirsty evangelists in the Americas. The process of Spanish evangelization was so awful that many Mayans fled to the mountains and the jungle to avoid persecution, and this led the Spanish officials to send a formal complaint to Spain because torture and death were paralyzing the economy. De Landa was criticized harshly by other priests and by the Spanish monarchy itself.

As in central Mexico, the Mayan population also suffered from smallpox and other diseases brought by the Europeans. When the city of Mérida was founded, there were less than 300,000 natives left on the peninsula, and by the year 1700 that number was only 130,000. Still, Yucatán was never subjugated completely, and large portions of its territory were not penetrated. The Spaniards could never subdue the inhabitants of the eastern part of the peninsula, where the entry of a white man meant almost certain death. That situation lasted in some regions even into the beginning of the 20th century, which is why the myth of the wild men of Yucatán still lead inhabitants to imagine a kind of monster that lived inside the jungle and devoured people.

The Colonial Era

"My beloved children, I do not know what you await to shake off the heavy yoke and laborious servitude in which the subjugation of the Spanish has placed you. I have traveled through all of the province and have inspected all of the villages and, considering carefully the usefulness the Spanish subjugation has brought to us, I have not found a single thing but painful and inexorable servitude.... The demand for tribute is not appeased by the poverty that locks up our comrades as in a jail, nor is the thirst for our blood satisfied by the continuous whippings that bite and tear our bodies to pieces." – Jacinto Canek

As the Spaniards began to make their way through the jungles of Belize, Chiapas and Guatemala, they realized that Yucatán was not an island, but part of the mainland that Cortés had already partially conquered. The main cities were founded in 1540 (Campeche), 1542 (Mérida) and 1543 (Valladolid), but Montejo's conquest was not easy. His expeditions were mainly formed by men who sought easy riches in the form of precious metals, but since the Yucatán lacks mountains and mineral deposits, the conquistadores, disappointed, deserted when they heard about gold found in Peru. Moreover, when the conquest seemed to be reaching a successful conclusion, the Mayans pushed the Spaniards back and nearly expelled them from the peninsula. Geography helped the natives, and extreme heat and lack of water complicated the task for the Europeans.

Unlike other parts of Mexico, the independent and strenuous spirit of the Mayans checked the impetus of the Spanish expeditions. The Spanish presence was countered by several wars, guerrillas, pirate incursions, and hunger from food shortages brought about by intense droughts.

One of the most important rebellions occurred in 1546, when the native priest, Chilam Anbal, presented himself as the Son of God. The Mayans, tired of the abuses and encouraged by the memories of their previous victories, crucified Spaniards and sent the amputated arms and legs of their former masters to other villages to invite them to join the rebellion. One writer noted, "The repudiation of the Maya towards Spanish domination went beyond slaughter and sacrifice. They destroyed and killed the domesticated animals and plants that the conquerors had brought from Europe. The natives who served in the homes of the Spaniards were executed too; they were killed by the rebels because they considered them traitors to their customs and their gods. The resistance movement lasted for four months, and during this time the Spaniards fought desperately to quell it. Finally, in March 1547, they crushed the last rebel town. The chief caciques and priests were executed or burned alive, including Chilam Anbal."[2]

100 years later, there was another rebellion during which the natives destroyed churches and Christian images. The Maya have a circular view of history, not linear, which meant they were certain that just as they had suffered defeat and subjugation, in time they would be free again.

---

[2] Sergio Quesada *et al*, *La colonización de los mayas peninsulares*, p. 43

In 1761, there was yet another rebellion, perhaps the most famous of all in the colonial era. This one was led by a legendary leader known as Canek, and though his uprising lasted only a few weeks, it had enormous symbolism and meaning, more related to cultural resistance than political demands. Originally called Jacinto Uc, he was born in Campeche in the middle of the 18th century, but he took the name of Canek, the last Itza monarch. He studied Latin and history in a Franciscan convent before he was expelled for his rebellious and impertinent temperament, and then he became a baker for several years. In a town in the center of the peninsula, he proclaimed that he was a king whose coming had been prophesied in the Bible, which earned him a whipping by the local priest. In the next town, when he was again scourged for his words, he presented himself as a reincarnation of Jesus Christ. On other occasions, he said he was Moctezuma II, the last Aztec emperor.

Robert W. Patch, a professor of the Department of History at Princeton University, wrote about this unique Mayan leader, "His actions speak of a man who believed in himself and conducted himself as a shaman. He traveled alone through the province as a beggar and fortune teller, and possibly attended the pagan rituals that took place in the mountains to the south, in the area beyond the Spanish control. He could also have wandered near Belize because he later claimed to have had contact with the English and that he had been brought to Yucatan on an English ship. He healed the sick and promised that with a sacred oil, made from pumpkin and honey, he would bring the dead back to life. Instead of meat, he ate jasmine flowers. He tried to convince others that he could fly."

Canek lived in a land conquered and supposedly pacified, but boiling in discontent due to the encomienda system implemented by Spain. As an indirect extension of Spanish rule, the practice of *encomienda* was introduced as a system of local patronage by which Spanish settlers were granted effective fiefdoms over certain regions and the subject populations within. According to the general regulations by which individual *encomendero* could function, they were responsible for the well-being and protection of the communities granted to them. Theoretically, in exchange for assuming responsibility for the religious conversion and training of the indigenous people, *encomendero* were granted the right to utilize the labor of the community for their own benefit.

The theory underpinning the *encomienda* system was relatively benign so far as Spanish colonization practices went, but the potential for abuse is quite obvious, and ultimately, the system came to be regarded as a de facto form of slavery, from which, in many instances, it was indistinguishable. Despite the cordiality of early encounters, the indigenous people under the *encomienda* suffered brutal exploitation at the hands of the Creole elite, and diseases brought by the foreigners began to ravage populations that had no immunity. The populations in the region declined so precipitously that by the late 16th century, the *encomienda* system had largely collapsed across much of Argentina. That said, in Paraguay, and in and around Asunción, which were isolated by Spain, the system continued, and in places where there were bountiful resources and well-established relationships, the system survived for generations in a mutually beneficial form.

Thus, as the ancestral lands of the natives were granted by the king to nobles of Spain or the church, the Mayans worked in semi-slavery, all the while watching their culture become systematically repressed. There were other situations that made the peninsula a fertile land for rebellion, such as the fact the tax charged to the natives was higher in Yucatán than the rest of Mexico.

Thus, one day in 1761, at the end of the Mass in the town of Cisteil, near Mérida, and apparently after an argument with the priest, Canek addressed the people in the Mayan language: "My beloved children, I do not know what you await to shake off the heavy yoke and laborious servitude in which the subjugation of the Spanish has placed you. I have traveled through all of the province and have inspected all of the villages and, considering carefully the usefulness the Spanish subjugation has brought to us, I have not found a single thing but painful and inexorable servitude.... The demand for tribute is not appeased by the poverty that locks up our comrades as in a jail, nor is the thirst for our blood satisfied by the continuous whippings that bite and tear our bodies to pieces."

Canek ordered all debts and tax receipts to be brought to him, and he proceeded to burn them in public. He then immediately ordered all the pigs to be sacrificed because they had the soul of the Spaniards. He was reputed to work miracles, affirmed that the triumph of the Maya was written in one of their sacred books, the *Chilam Balam*, and finally proclaimed himself as king of the Maya with a crown taken from a statue of the Virgin Mary in the local church. On the day of his coronation, his followers went to the church and destroyed the images. People kissed his feet and hands when they approached him. The fact that the ephemeral king declared that the Mayans were to marry Spanish women, and that he himself would be the first to choose a wife among them, means that more than the extermination of the Spaniards, he was looking for the conquerors to be assimilated, just like two centuries before, when the shipwrecked Gonzalo Guerrero had become one of them and taken a Mayan wife and children.

When Canek and his people started the uprising, his fame spread throughout the peninsula. Crowds came to see if he was really a king. His followers fought with sticks, machetes, and a few guns, but most importantly, they fought with messianic fervor. Canek proclaimed that he was God's envoy, so naturally, his words scandalized the religious authorities. The news ran throughout Yucatán, and other local natives participated in acts of passive resistance when they heard of the monarch who had established his court in the town's church.

Canek's forces annihilated the first squad of 20 soldiers sent to subdue him, and that prompted the governor of Yucatán to send all the available military might. Meanwhile, the rebels sent letters to all the nearby towns, including Uxmal, asking for help. Canek encouraged his people by telling them that the Miskito would come to aid them.

In the end, the authorities of Mérida repressed the uprising with characteristically ferocious violence. On November 26, 1761, more than 500 Maya were burned alive and more than 1,500 were arrested, destined to be executed at a later date. The Spanish captains testified afterwards that the natives had fallen in the battlefield without making a single sound, for Canek had promised them that if they did not "move their lips" (screaming or crying), they would not die.

Canek fled to the south of the peninsula, where he was able to gather another 300 men, but he was again defeated, and when he was captured in Sibac, he was sentenced to be tortured to death. The rebellion had barely lasted less than a month before the rebellious leader was burned alive and had his ashes thrown into the wind. After his death, the Mayans were forbidden to carry weapons, participate in public celebrations, or even play their music. The town of Cisteil, where everything had started, was erased from the face of the Earth and covered with salt.

The Five Star Republic

Until the end of the colonial era, Yucatán continued as a captaincy of New Spain, indirectly subject to the viceroy and linked more to Spain and the colony of Cuba than to Mexico. The territory was frequently harassed by French and English pirates, who attacked various islands and ports off the eastern coast of the peninsula and occasionally made inland incursions. In the midst of these campaigns, which were often sponsored by Great Britain, the British colony of British Honduras was established in modern Belize. The British wanted part of Central America in order to exploit the dye stick for the textile industry, along with wood. Although the governments of Yucatán often pushed into British Honduras, the colony was finally recognized as a result of the Spanish-British alliance against Napoleon at the start of the 19th century.

As the 19th century quickly brought the Napoleonic Wars, the New World colonies took advantage of Spain's devastation to revolt. From the ashes of the Spanish Empire would rise new nations, with new borders and new problems. Lacking the infrastructure or commercial ties to properly suppress the colonial revolts, Spain would see its massive empire dissolve in the wake of the Napoleonic Wars.

The natural progression of it all was a greater sense of pending independence across the American colonies, each of which experienced autonomy to a greater or lesser extent. Some recognized the Spanish regency while others did not, but all to a greater or lesser extent challenged the authority of royal officials who sought to govern on behalf of the Spanish regency. Numerous factions evolved between royalists and anti-royalisst, and those advocating independence and those remaining loyal. Even though all of the various juntas carefully carried out their actions in the name of the deposed King Ferdinand VII, their simple existence presented the opportunity for those favoring complete independence to air their views both publicly and safely. The independence advocates, adopting nationalist positions, referred to themselves as "patriots," after which the fault lines tended to run between the patriots and the royalists, with the former enjoying a growing majority.

The situation in the southern regions of South America was confused. Peru, the traditional heartland of the Spanish Empire in the New World, declared for the Council of Regency, while in the Viceroyalty of New Grenada, revolutionary juntas were proclaimed in a number of provincial cities. The most radical of these was the junta of Caracas, which fell under the control of radical Republicans like Francisco de Miranda and Simón Bolívar. In Chile, after some hesitation, a revolutionary junta established itself in Santiago.

Miranda

Although the Viceroyalty of Río de la Plata effectively collapsed and was replaced by the "United Provinces of the Río de la Plata," and in its capital of Buenos Aires the Primera Junta superficially declared its loyalty to Ferdinand VII, bitter divisions continued to exist. While Buenos Aires adopted a revolutionary, independent position, other provincial cities such as Montevideo, Córdoba, La Paz, and Asunción all accepted the authority of Cádiz, triggering what came to be known as the Argentine War of Independence.

These conflicts were reflected across the spectrum of Spanish-speaking territories in the Americas, all responding to the same political stimulus. In addition, the uncertainty and insecurity of the moment triggered multiple other disturbances involving Indians, blacks, and mestizos, each responding to opportunities presented by a vacuum of legitimate government.

The two main regions of military conflict were Mexico, where a nativist rebellion erupted in

1810 under the leadership of a Creole priest by the name of Miguel Hidalgo, and the Río de la Plata region. The ostensibly royalist Primera Junta very quickly fell under the influence of a group of Jacobin radicals led by a liberal lawyer, journalist, and translator of Rousseau's *Social Contract* named Mariano Moreno. The Junta opened the Port of Buenos Aires to international trade, going so far as to proclaim the equality of all citizens of the provinces regardless of race or origin. These egalitarian principals, however, disguised the reality that the Junta served the narrow interests of the *Porteños*, the elite urban dwellers of the city and the landed nobility of the countryside. Metropolitan Spanish merchants were marginalized, and no outsider was included in government.

Moreno

Napoleon's forces had been devastated by his invasion of Russia, and shortly after he was defeated at Leipzig in October 1813, he abdicated the French throne. In conjunction with hat, British forces led by the Duke of Wellington took back the Iberian Peninsula from the French, which led to the restoration of the Bourbons and the reclamation of the Spanish throne by Ferdinand VII. The first thing Charles IV did once the hue and cry of celebration had died down was to try and reestablish his authority both over Spain and the rest of the empire. He returned Spain to the absolute rule of the monarchy, reinstated the Inquisition and the Jesuits, and generally reversed many of the earlier Bourbon Reforms, blaming them for the political indiscipline at home and in the colonies. As one historian, Stanley Payne, described him, "He proved in many ways the basest king in Spanish history. Cowardly, selfish, grasping, suspicious, and vengeful, [he] seemed almost incapable of any perception of the commonwealth. He thought only in terms of his power and security and was unmoved by the enormous sacrifices of Spanish people to retain their independence and preserve his throne."

Ferdinand VII

The king's moral failings aside, the prospects for reestablishing royal authority in the colonies were good. The uprising in Mexico was over, New Grenada was back in the fold, and Buenos Aires' Primera Junta had manifestly failed to consolidate its rule over the interior provinces. There seemed no reason to suppose that a well provisioned and supported Spanish army could not sail west from Europe and whip the colonies back into line. The tide appeared to have turned against the forces of independence in Central America and South America, and notwithstanding the success of the American Revolution, the Catholic monarchy of Spain would maintain its grip on the political future of the Indies until at least the 1820s. With a strong monarchy back in place, political opposition could no longer be construed as anti-French, but simply treason. Edwin Williamson, a historian of Latin America, explained, "As in the period 1808-1810, the majority of creoles had to choose between embracing the devil of absolutism, which they at least knew, and taking a stride into the unknown behind a small number of squabbling radicals." [3]

[3] Williamson, Edwin. *The Penguin History of Latin America*. (Penguin Books, London, 1992) p221

With the imminent fall of Spanish rule in America, other European countries also began to covet the vast and uninhabited territories of northern Mexico. Although the Mexican rebels were wiped out by the Spanish army, in 1821 the criollos organized a coup d'état against their parents´ country and declared independence from New Spain. Mexico´s first ruler was an emperor named Agustin de Iturbide, and a map of his domains would have aroused the envy of Alexander the Great. Mexico now spanned from Panama in the south to Oregon, almost 5,000 miles from border to border, making it larger than Alexander´s empire.

However, the only thing that was impressive about the Mexican empire was its size, as many territories were unoccupied and belonged to it only by name. Most of the population lived in the south and the porous northern border was more a mirage than a reality. In 1821, Mexico possessed about 3 million square miles for just 6 million inhabitants, but in the empire of Agustin I, the political, economic and cultural life thrived around the capital, Mexico City.

Agustin de Iturbide

When Mexico became independent in 1821 after years of fighting, the independence of Yucatán was secured peacefully, and virtually automatically. The governor summoned the civil, military and ecclesiastical authorities, and after a brief presentation, he declared the independence of Yucatán and announced the desire to become a part of the new nation. After the overthrow of the first ruler of independent Mexico, Emperor Agustín de Iturbide, the rebel soldier Antonio López de Santa Anna, who would give the country many headaches in the following decades, tried to succeed him. However, instead of assuming the title of Antonio I as he wanted, he was sent to be governor of Yucatán, the poorest state in the republic, which was in effect an exile.

Santa Anna

Making the most of it, Santa Anna took the opportunity to befriend the Yucatecans, who made him their governor. As one contemporary writer put it, "The people of Campeche spoon-feed him to attract him, and the Yucatecans flatter him to win his affection. Copious meals and balls, cockfights and mestizas, where the commander goes wild and sins, morning, afternoon and night. He orders according to the instructions he is carrying; but he turns a blind eye so that no one will listen. And he goes from celebration to celebration throughout the province."

Governor Santa Anna realized that many of the merchants and elite of Yucatán felt closer to Cuba, and therefore to Spain, than to Mexico. Yucatán depended on its trade with Spain and the Caribbean, but Mexico had ordered all states to suspend trade with Spain and its colonies, and that meant cutting off Yucatán's main source of income. The ruling class in Mérida wanted to reverse independence, rejoin the Spanish Empire, or declare itself as a separate republic to ensure friendly ties with Cuba and Spain.

Santa Anna asked the Mexican government to lift the ban on trade in Yucatán, but the government did not see things his way. Santa Anna, in a characteristic display of his ability to think in grandiose terms, concluded that the only way trade with the island would not be interrupted would be to conquer Cuba and free it from Spanish rule. For that, he would lead a liberating expedition, in the style of Simón Bolívar and José de San Martín, so he gathered 5,000 men and prepared to sail in August 1824, having heard the news that there was discontent on the island. According to his calculations, the Cubans would welcome him as a savior and support the landing of his troops. However, Spain learned of the plans and fortified the island, leading the Mexicans to call off the plans and ensuring the Spanish would hold Cuba until the end of the Spanish-American War.

The Republic of Yucatán

In 1836, the Mexican province of Texas successfully revolted and became an independent republic, a chapter of Mexican history that Santa Anna actually remains best known for as a result of his siege of the Alamo. Texas formally asked to be annexed by the United States in 1845, understandably angering the Mexican government, which still considered Texas to be part of its territory. Mexico had previously warned that the annexation of Texas would cause Mexico to declare war on the United States, and a few years later, the Mexican-American War would end with the United States taking a vast amount of territory from Mexico, including California the very year gold was discovered there.

Following Texas' example, Yucatán would attempt to secede from Mexico in 1841. A year earlier, a centralist system had been established in Mexico, which meant the states lost their sovereignty and became departments. It also meant their governors would be appointed directly by the president, and local armies would lose their autonomy. In addition to this, export taxes were increased in Yucatán, and the province was required to send soldiers to fight the Texas Revolution.

On October 1, 1841, the Yucatán's local Congress declared relations with Mexico broken, and a project to decree the total independence of Yucatán was presented to the legislature, which it approved. In retaliation, the Mexican government blocked the ports of the peninsula.

The governor of Yucatán was ordered to remove all the flags of Mexico and to raise those of the new republic. The new flag was vaguely reminiscent of the United States: a green field to symbolize independence, red and white stripes, and five stars representing the five divisions of Yucatán (Mérida, Izamal, Valladolid, Tekax and Campeche).

The flag

Like Texas, Yucatán had extensive coasts facing the Gulf of Mexico, and therefore the peninsula a direct connection with Texas by sea without the need to cut across Mexican land. Both republics, Yucatán and Texas, quickly established diplomatic relations and signed friendship and commerce treaties. There was a diplomatic representation for Texas in Mérida, and one for Yucatán in Austin. The second president of Texas, Mirabeau B. Lamar, secretly negotiated with Yucatán to ally against Mexico. Texas still had a tenuous grasp on independence, and Lamar figured that a slong as Mexico was kept busy trying to quell the separatist attempts in the peninsula, it would leave Texas alone.

Lamar

Yucatán also made provisions. In 1841, it agreed to pay $8,000 a month to Texas to defend the Yucatecan coasts against the Mexicans, and if either side took loot from captured Mexican ships, both republics would divide it equally. Although the Texan ships briefly patrolled the Yucatecan coast, they never went into combat with the Mexicans.

Santa Anna, now Mexico's president, tried to bend Yucatán to his will by force. There were clashes in mid-1842, and national troops were defeated and forced to capitulate in Tixpéhual, but the Republic of Yucatán was mostly isolated, and its leaders eventually determined it was favorable to rejoin Mexico as long as certain conditions were met. In 1843, the republic's forces defeated Mexican forces once again, and this time it took advantage of that opportunity to negotiate its return to Mexico's fold.

The Caste War

"Slavery in Mexico! Yes, I found it. I found it first in Yucatán." – John Kenneth Turner

Just a few years later, Yucatán's leaders again became dissatisfied with the Mexican government's inability to meet the conditions, and they declared the Yucatán independent once more in 1846, the same year the Mexican-American War broke out between the United States and Mexico. During that conflict, Yucatán decided to stay neutral so that its maritime trade was not jeopardized. The United States, already at war with Mexico, occupied the island of Carmen and threatened to block the ports of the Peninsula, but the people of Campeche reminded the Americans that they were neutral, and they were able to convince the Americans to stop blocking maritime traffic.

This time, however, Yucatán´s plans for independence would be upended by indigenous people who had been living in the peninsula all along. In 1847, as Mexico had its capital occupied by General Winfield Scott, an internal rebellion broke out in Yucatán among the Maya, who, despite mostly being forgotten and entirely overlooked, still comprised a vast majority of the population in the region. The ensuing conflict, now known as the Caste War of Yucatán, was to be the last great act of indigenous resistance in the Americas, and it was certainly the most comprehensive rebellion among the Maya since the years immediately after the arrival of the Spanish.

This Mayan attempt to reconquer their territory and autonomy began on July 18, 1847. That day, a number of Maya, provided with viand and weapons, gathered on the property of a man named Jacinto Pat, about 25 miles from the city of Valladolid. When the Yucatán authorities were warned that an uprising was forming, they captured one of the leaders, Manuel Antonio Ay. He had been discovered by a bartender who was serving him in his tavern and found a letter hidden in his hat detailing the plans for the insurrection. According to some testimonies, the plan was to slaughter all whites, to proclaim the independence of the natives, and to crown Cecilio Chi as Lord of the Mayans. Ay was shot in the main square of Valladolid, but Jacinto Pat and Cecilio Chi were able to flee.

A portrait of Chi

In retaliation, government forces set fire to the town of Tepich without allowing the elderly, women, and children to leave their houses. According to Nelson Reed, "The fears of the Ladinos (whites and mestizos) turned a political and social revolution into a racial conflict, and thereby caused sadism and savagery on both sides."[4] The next day, Chi's men killed all the whites and mestizos, save for a few women, who were then raped. The ruthless violence perpetrated on all sides was an omen of things to come as the Maya launched what ended up being the largest indigenous uprising in the Americas.

Even before Mexico's independence, the colonization of the peninsula and lucrative cultivation of henequen had been achieved at the cost of absorbing, confiscating, and stealing land from the Mayans. The dispossession had started back in the 18th century, when the landowners "denounced" vacant lands, usually territory of the communities, and expelled the peasants through strong-arm tactics and violence. Many peoples thus lost their livelihoods. As the 19th century progressed, the communities disappeared under the weight of peonage, dispossession, and destitution, confining the peasant class to large henequen plantations. Some henequen kings owned up to 23,000 square miles of land, in effect establishing their own small kingdoms, and the natives were tied to the estate or hacienda where they worked. In exchange for a hut, a small piece of land, and a day of brutal work, they served the master from sunrise to sunset.

---

[4] Nelson Reed, *La guerra de castas de Yucatán.*

This situation was aggravated by the immense taxes that the government and the church imposed. When the peasants did not pay the weekly tax to the Catholic temples, the political authorities persecuted them, and after receiving several lashes, they were sent to prison. The tensions were further exacerbated by an 1847 law which deprived them of their status as citizens and reduced them to servants, much the way they were before Mexican independence. According to the ruling class, the natives had shown no ability to exercise their constitutional rights and obligations, and therefore they deserved the persecution.

In 1908, American journalist John Kenneth Turner visited Yucatán, and though the things he saw shocked him, they had been ongoing for several generations. Kenneth, a fervent socialist and believer in the Mayan revolution, has been accused of exaggeration in his work, but based on what he described in his book, *Barbarous Mexico*, the situation that led to the Caste War was so desperate that it led the Mayans to launch a war of extermination.

Turner

Around half a million people inhabited the peninsula when the Caste War began, and Turner estimated that 95% of the population was Mayan, although this figure seems inflated. Richmond offered a figure of 75% Indian and 10% mestizos, but either way, it's clear the indigenous people numbered in the hundreds of thousands, and Yucatán's economy depended on large-scale production of henequen, which was exported to the United States and England. Henequen, also known as "sisal," is an agave that does not require much water and adapts well to the thin soils of Yucatán. The Mayans used it before the Spanish Conquest to produce ropes, hammocks, rough fabrics, sandals, baskets, bags, and to distill alcoholic beverages. In the 18th century, the Spaniards discovered the uses of the plant, and soon the agaves covered the land. The harvest required many arms and was an intensive labor task that required several hours of labor per plant. Once the fibers were dry, the laborers could make high resistance ropes, which were useful for navigation.

Turner visited a plantation of about 1,500 workers, and all were dressed in straw hats and went barefoot, with poor clothing. Of the workers, half were men fit for hard work, while the rest were women and children, who also worked to help the family since the man had to meet a quota. At the end of the day they received a credit of 25 cents for the hacienda store, ensuring they could only spend the money on goods produced there. In the store, they could buy corn, beans, salt, chili peppers, clothes and blankets. Turner explained, "Here and there among them I saw tired-looking women and children, sometimes little girls as young as eight or ten. Two thousand leaves a day is the usual stint on San Antonio Yaxché. On other plantations I was told that it is sometimes as high as three thousand. 'We come to work gladly,' said another young Maya, 'because we're starved to it. But before the end of the first week we want to run away. That is why they lock us up at night.'" The day began at 4 o'clock in the morning when the bell rang, and ended when daylight ended. On Sundays the people rested, and the only distraction for men was to get drunk after going to Mass. Sometimes people were allowed to visit family or friends in other plantations, but never to marry outside the hacienda since that would require the sale of the "slave," as Turner calls them. The transaction was not officially the sale of a slave, but his debt which men carried for generations. In practical terms, their situation was equivalent to slavery. "The planters do not call their chattels slaves. They call them 'people,' or 'laborers,' especially when speaking to strangers. But when speaking confidentially they have said to me: 'Yes, they are slaves.'"

Turner recounted stories of natives being beaten to death, and he claimed the first thing he saw on a henequen plantation was a "slave" being whipped 50 times with a wet rope. "I saw no punishments worse than beating in Yucatán," he wrote. Women were forced to kneel when they were whipped. He reported, "The farms are so large that each has a little city of its own, inhabited by from 500 to 2,500 people, according to the size of the farm. The owners of these great farms are the chief slave-holders of Yucatán; the inhabitants of the little cities are the slaves."

As soon as the Caste War began, it promised to be bloody. Taking a page out of the authorities' playbook, whenever the rebels took a town or village, they slaughtered the population. In fact, it was common for them to kill men with machetes, even when they had guns at hand. In retaliation, Mayan homes were burned by the government forces.

For the first time in centuries, authorities were at a loss to contain the natives. The *chilam Balam*, a compilation of sacred texts, gave the war a messianic character. Part of it read, "Only because of the crazy times, because of the crazy priests, was that sadness came to us, that Christianity entered us. Then was the beginning of our misery, the beginning of alms, the cause of hidden discord, the beginning of fights with guns, the beginning of abuse, the beginning of spoils in every way, the beginning of our slavery to debts, the beginning of the debts stuck to our backs, the beginning of continuous brawl, the beginning of suffering. It was the beginning of the work of the Spaniards, the fathers and the blood suckers of the poor Indian. The day will come when the tears of your eyes will come to God and the justice of God will come down in a single blow over the world. It is truly God's will that Ah-Kantenal and Ix-Pucyolá (destructive deities) return to gnaw them from the surface of the Earth. Itzam will wake up!"

The Caste War would last 55 years, and the underlying problems that originated it would continue to be a cause for concern until 1937, but as early as September 1847, a couple of months after the first fighting, the government offered amnesty to the rebels who submitted. The authorities thought that this was simply another temporary revolt, despite the fact unprecedented cruelty reigned on both sides. For example, on a Yaxché ranch, the natives opened the chest of a child in the presence of its mother and, in the manner of the ancient Mayan priests, drank the child's blood, exhibited the child's heart, and ate it. On the other side, a priest surnamed Herrera liked to put his saddle on any Mayan prisoner in the vicinity, mount him, whip him, and wound his belly with the spikes. The government eventually erected a pillory to torture the suspects of the conspiracy, sent most of the chieftains to prison in Campeche, and hung one of them, Alejandro Tzab, by the ears to make him confess. The natives, although well-equipped with firearms, preferred to kill with machetes, including murdering Catholic priests.

The first stage of the war, which witnessed the seemingly unstoppable advance of the Mayans, lasted until July 1848, and whites, mestizos, and blacks were exterminated in more than 250 villages. By that point, about two-thirds of the peninsula was dominated by the rebels, and the army retreated to the gates of Mérida, the capital of Yucatán.

The Yucatán government was so alarmed that it sent the most important scholar and journalist in the region, Justo Sierra O'Reilly, to Washington to ask for help from the United States, and to even concede the sovereignty of Yucatán in exchange for military aid to extinguish the Mayan rebellion. President Polk received him at the White House, where Sierra told him that the Mayans were on a mission to destroy civilization itself. On April 29, Polk communicated to Congress, "It appears that the Indians of Yucatan are waging a war of extermination against the white race. In this civil war, they spare neither age, nor sex, but put to death, indiscriminately, all who fall within their power. The inhabitants, panic-stricken, and destitute of arms, are flying before their savage pursuers towards the coast, and their expulsion from their country, or their extermination would seem to be inevitable, unless they can obtain assistance from abroad. In this condition, they have, through their constituted authorities, implored the aid of this government, to save them from destruction, offering, in case this should be granted, to transfer the dominion and sovereignty of the peninsula to the United States."

O'Reilly

Polk

Political intrigues and rivalries in America prevented the two sides from reaching an agreement, so O'Reilly returned to Mérida without a deal on August 17, 1848, the same day Yucatán's governor decreed the peninsula would be returned to Mexico. Despite that, the situation remained desperate as the Mexican government did not send help. The governor of Yucatán subsequently offered the peninsula to Spain, provided that the Spanish occupied it and subdued the Maya, and then to Britain, which also did not take the offer because it threatened conflict with the United States. Instead, the British established a weapons post near Bacalar to sell guns to the Mayans, and the British ordered the authorities of British Honduras to protect the indigenous people. By recognizing them as belligerents, it promised to give them "all the guarantees corresponding to the friend nations of Great Britain."

As the negotiations failed to bear fruit, the white population, near the point of hysteria, fled to the main cities of the peninsula, to the islands, and to Belize, leaving their homes and land.

Meanwhile, the government awarded medals to outstanding soldiers for "their adherence and loyalty to the white race."

On April 19, 1848, after tense negotiations in the jungle, representatives of the governor and Jacinto Pat signed the Tzucacab agreement. The treaty stated that the personal tax would be abolished, the tax for baptism and marriage would be reduced, the natives would get authorization to use the communal land and the mountains without paying rent, the servants' debts in the haciendas would be canceled, and all the rifles that had been collected would be returned to the Mayans. The tax on distilled spirits was eliminated as well. Pat was named governor of all the natives, and the governor of Yucatán would be a lifetime governor.

However, the agreement did not have the expected effects. Cecilio Chi, the leader of the indigenous people in the east, desired the total extermination of the white race and was not happy with the lifetime appointment of Pat.

By mid-1848 the Maya controlled almost the entire peninsula, with the exception of Mérida and Campeche, and even there the populations felt unsafe. Most families moved downtown for protection inside the city walls, and in the port of Campeche, an American ship was ready to evacuate American citizens. When Mérida was surrounded, the governor tried to order an evacuation, but he couldn't find paper in his office to print the proclamation. Nelson Reed described the scene: "Rumors ran through the streets that savages were everywhere. People escaped to the sea from (the port of) Sisal, Campeche or any other port where they could grab anything that floated, to take them anywhere. Citizens forgot about *Gringo Go Home* and made requests for protection. In the streets of Merida and Campeche there was talk of general slaughter, elimination of the white population of Yucatan, which meant more than 140 thousand people, counting the mestizos."[5]

Just when the apocalypse seemed imminent, the terrified whites discovered that the Maya had suddenly left. As it turned out, a cloud of winged ants appeared, which for the Mayans announced the beginning of the rains. Therefore, it was time to return to the crops. Years later, the son of one of the leaders explained to historian E.H. Thompson, "It was scorching heat. Suddenly there appeared the *sh'mataneheeles* (winged ants) in great clouds from the north, south, east and west, all over the place. When they saw this, those with my father said to each other, and said to their brothers, 'Ehen! The time has come for us to do our plantation, because if we do not do it, we will not have the Grace of God to fill our children's belly.' Thus they said and argued, and thought a lot, and when the morning came, my father's men said each one to his batab: 'I'm leaving.' And despite the pleas and threats of the bosses, each man rolled up his blanket and prepared his food bag, tightened the straps of his sandals and set off towards his house and his cornfield. Then the Batabob, knowing that it was useless to attack the city with the few remaining men, met in council and decided to go back home." If Mérida, the capital of

---

[5] Nelson Reed

Yucatán, had fallen, things may have been different, and perhaps the control of the Mayans over the peninsula would have been complete.

After the summer of 1848, Mexican and Yucatán authorities took the initiative on all fronts. Reinforced by the federation, the army advanced towards the center and south of the peninsula and took back important places. New atrocities occurred during that campaign, as soldiers took natives by their hands and feet, rocked them into the air, and caught them with bayonets. The Maya, in turn, took white children by the ankles and whipped them to the ground.

The shipment of natives as slaves to the plantations of Cuba also began "under the auspices of the government." In February 1849, shipments began at 25 pesos per head, with the justification that there was hunger and the state could not feed so many prisoners. Since they were rebels, authorities actually suggested they were doing the prisoners a favor, and in turn, Yucatán would receive badly needed resources. This slave trade aroused serious criticism, especially from the consul of Mexico in Havana, who communicated the news to Mexico City.

By May 1849, Cecilio Chi and Jacinto Pat had been murdered, the Mayans had been expelled from the west of the peninsula, and they were beating a general retreat south towards the jungle. Their poverty actually facilitated the exodus since their huts could be built elsewhere and they only had to carry their few belongings in their arms. Venancio Pec and Florentino Chan took over, and when in October the civil and ecclesiastical authorities offered a peace agreement, they responded that it would only be possible if the government troops stopped "doing evil to the Indians," who would never submit again to Mérida because they preferred to follow orders from the British. They claimed to have received many services and benefits from the British (weapons), and that they would appoint their kings and run their government according to their customs. They offered as proof of their sincerity that they had not gone out to seek a fight with the whites, in accordance with Queen Victoria's instructions.

Belize's superintendent, Charles St. John Fancourt, met with Venancio Pec and Florentino Chan at Ascension Bay to try to serve as an intermediary with the Yucatán government. He heard the complaints of the Indians about injustices, abuses, and taxes, and their precondition that the Mayans would only accept peace if they got full independence in the territory they occupied. Pec communicated to Fancourt his desire to be under the sovereignty of Great Britain and asked to meet Queen Victoria.

Reluctant to surrender, the rebels retreated towards the uninhabited jungle of eastern Yucatán, but it seemed that they had lost their momentum. Little did they know that the real spirit of the movement was about to start blowing.

In 1850, both sides seemed to have reached a stalemate, and they had done so at a tremendous cost, as the population of Yucatán, according to the 1850 census, had been cut in half. Then something happened that would give the Caste War its legendary quality: the appearance of a talking cross.

One afternoon in the middle of 1850, a Mayan leader named José María Barrera took his tired group to a dense point in the jungle, near the modern border with Belize. In a ravine he found a 15-foot deep cenote with crystalline waters and a large tree, where, according to oral tradition, he saw a small wooden cross barely 10 centimeters long. Barrera put it on a hillside where the Mayans could see it and pray for the end of oppression. It was said that the cross spoke.

Soon the word of this finding spread, and it was significant because it had taken place at a place considered sacred (a cenote), and the cross reminded them of the Mayan symbolism of pre-Hispanic times. The talking cross reportedly told the Mayans that it would make them invincible and the war should continue. People came near to hear the cross, and thus a powerful religious movement began to take form, a mixture of Christianity and the ancestral religion of the Maya. To them, the cross was the voice of God giving orders and telling them which places to attack.

With that, the Caste War became a theocratic movement, and it offered an excellent example of syncretism. For the Maya, the stick symbolized the first tree in the universe, and the arms represented the Earth as the boundary between the heavens and the underworld. The people built huts around the cenote, which soon became a small city, and then the new capital of the Mayan nation. The followers of the cross, who believed they were waging a holy war, called themselves the "cruzob," a surprising name similar to the "crusaders" of the Middle Ages. By the end of 1850, a sanctuary to the talking cross was erected, and people came to hear the cross speak in their pre-Hispanic language.[6]

With that, the third stage of the war had begun, and this period was characterized by the consolidation and stabilization of the areas being held by both sides, serious political crises for the local government, and occasional expeditions against the Maya. Since the border with Belize was left unguarded, the British settlers had continued exploiting precious woods and dye sticks on the banks of the Hondo River and the southern tip of Chetumal Bay, which was part of Yucatán's territory. This also allowed the Maya to maintain contact with the British and acquire weapons and supplies.

Meanwhile, the Maya created a new population at the site of the talking cross, about 10 miles from the Ascension Bay, which they called *Chan* Santa Cruz (Little Santa Cruz), today the city of Felipe Carrillo Puerto. Following the instructions of the talking cross, the Maya attacked Kampocolché, and although they were nearly victorious despite their blind faith, they were eventually defeated.

In the wake of that fighting, Colonel Juan María Novelo heard from the prisoners of the birth

---

[6] Most historians believe that a ventriloquist named Manuel Nahuat was helping Barrera. When Nahuat died in battle, the cross stopped speaking to the people and began dictating letters.

of the new religion. He immediately attacked the place, and his soldiers were amazed to find a town of more than 1,000 people where just a short while earlier there was only jungle. Manuel Nahuat died in the battle, and he was the one credited with making the cross speak. Colonel Novelo, like the evangelizers of old, destroyed the sanctuary and took away the cross and other relics.

Thereafter, a three-cross set designed to replace the original, stopped speaking and began dictating letters that circulated throughout the area. The cross demanded its enemies to return the land to their rightful owners. The letters were signed by the interpreter Juan de la Cruz Puc, secretary of Barrera and new priest of the nascent religion. The Maya dressed the crosses with huipiles, skirts and colored ribbons. To keep the fight alive, Barrera installed a thatched-roof church and dug a well behind the altar where a person hid inside a wooden vault in order to amplify his voice. Barrera died in 1852, but the cult of the cross continued.

The British Empire was the first nation to recognize the independent Mayan state of Chan Santa Cruz, which comprised approximately the modern state of Quintana Roo, a region that stretched from Tulum (near present-day Cancun) to the Belize border. The recognition came thanks to the significant volume of foreign trade between British Honduras and the Mayan territory.

In 1855, Yucatán had seemed to reach a point of exhaustion and declared peace. Officials considered the uprising more than a racial war, as the movement had become a confrontation between Mexico and Chan Santa Cruz, the first indigenous nation to exist since the arrival of Europeans in the 15th century. Nelson Reed noted, "Of all the indigenous rebellions since the araguacos fired their arrows against Columbus's sailors, this was the only one that had succeeded."

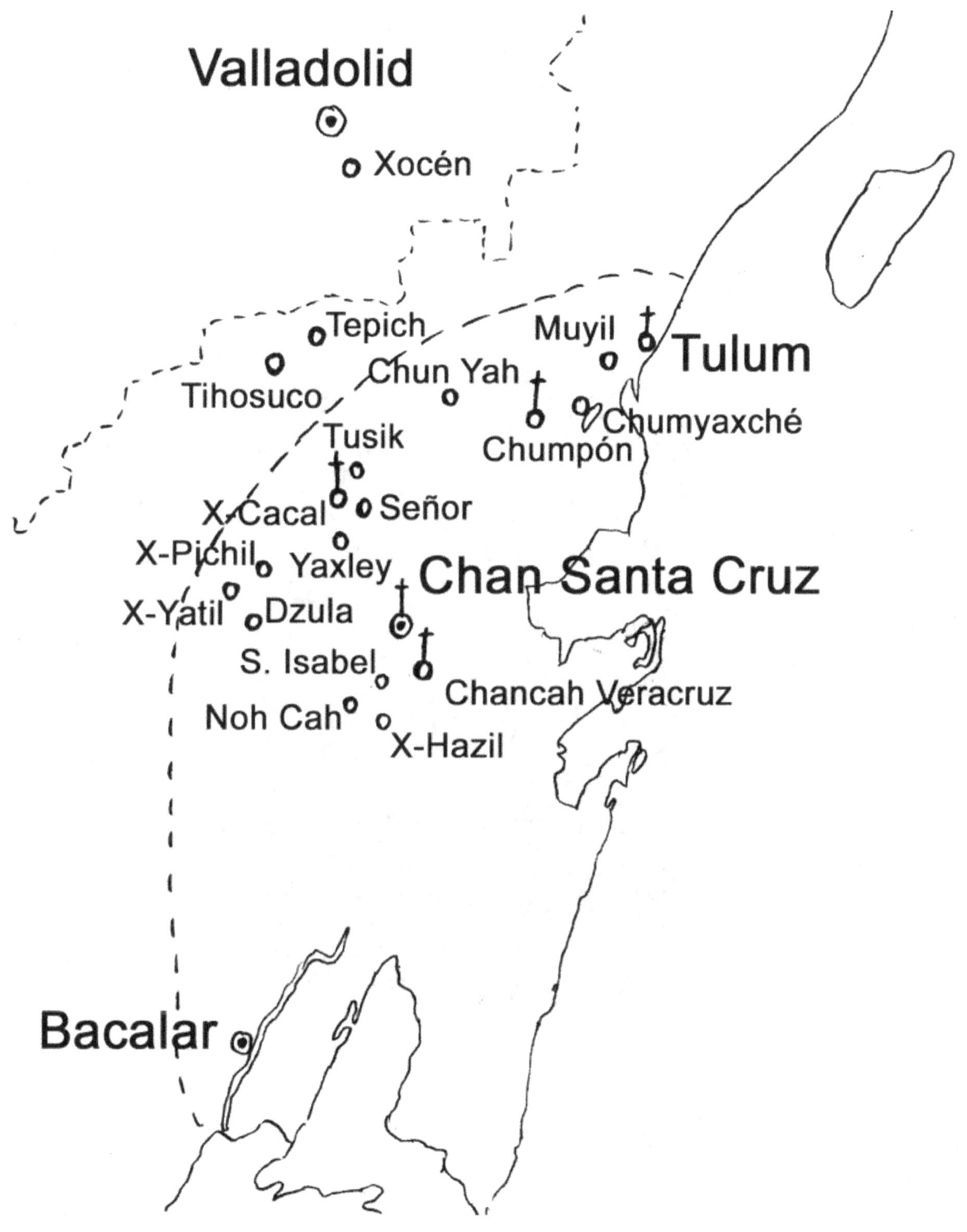

A map of the region in 1870

In the following years, Yucatán and Mexico did not give up trying to subdue the Mayans. On January 2, 1860, Governor Agustín Acereto organized a new expedition against Chan Santa Cruz, which was occupied on January 12. His troops, however, were decimated by the indigenous guerrillas, to the point that only 600 of 3,000 men survived.

The war was slowly attenuated as the Maya began to be employed in the henequen farms, where increasing production was able to mitigate the rigors of servitude. The other determining factor for pacification was that Britain agreed to stop selling weapons to the Maya. The support had allowed the British to consolidate their commercial activity in the Caribbean and to pressure Mexico to sign a treaty of limits with British Honduras, which they finally achieved in 1893. Mexico yielded 23,000 square kilometers to the British, and the definitive establishment of the border allowed President Porfirio Díaz to send Othón P. Blanco to the peninsula to enforce the dividing line and prevent arms trafficking.

Diaz

The final surrender of the Maya would be the work of General Ignacio A. Bravo, a veteran of the war against France, who arrived in 1899 as head of the military zone. By this point, the Maya were locked by the sea in the east, by the British in the south, and Yucatán in the north. With no more provisions from the British, who were now more interested in their increasing trade with Mexico than in the small nation of Santa Cruz, and under pressure from the Mexican state, the Maya reached a fatal impasse. General Bravo's final campaign was a slow but systematic advance with a new terrible weapon, the machine gun, that caused horror among the Mayans, who could avoid a single shot with their machetes but could obviously not do so against machine guns. The resistance of the Maya, which had lasted more than 50 years, was coming to an end.

Bravo

The chiefs of the different regions met in Chan Santa Cruz, and after seeing their lack of gunpowder, ammunition, and corn, they decided to set fire to the village and disperse in small groups. They entered the jungle and agreed to meet again every full moon at a fixed place.

In 1901, General Bravo took the town of San José de Santa Cruz on May 5 without firing a single shot, as the Maya had also destroyed that town. Bravo mistakenly thought that he had captured Chan Santa Cruz, so he renamed the village as Santa Cruz de Bravo (now Felipe Carrillo Puerto). In fact, neither Bravo nor the government knew the location of Chan Santa Cruz, the last organized stronghold of the Maya, because nothing was left of it.

Quintana Roo

The new regime hastened to turn Santa Cruz de Bravo into a "civilized" city. As one writer explained, "The schools that flanked the church became barracks, with a main square surrounded by thatched roof constructions; warehouses and shops bordered the square, where they planted orange trees and built a fence, walks, benches and a fountain made of stone. For the telegraph and electric light a generator had been installed; a pump carried water from the cenote to a tank; warehouses and workshops were built. Due to indifference, or in order to leave bad times behind, the church was not used as it was. The main entrance was sealed with bricks and made a prison inside for the convicted workers, male and female; they were locked up together and left abandoned for nights of rape or murder. They couldn't have desecrated the church more. Certainly, civilization had arrived."

Although this officially ended the Caste War, the Maya continued the guerrilla war. The governor of Yucatán wrote to President Díaz in 1901, "Of course and without hesitation I recognize that Yucatan has not been able, on its own, in more than half a century, to recover, pacify and hold, let alone colonize and promote the southeast region, segregated fifty-three years ago by the Mayan rebellion (...) and I firmly believe that only the Nation is in a position to obtain those benefits. But since these cannot be implemented with the necessary freedom of action and efficiency, as long as the reconquered zone remains under the state's jurisdiction, the convenience of erecting it in the Federal Territory is evident."

Given this situation, President Díaz finally decided to segment the peninsula, removing the Mayan territory from the state of Yucatán and turning it into a federal territory, which was named Quintana Roo. The namesake was Andrés Quintana Roo, an old freedom fighter from the time of the Mexican fight for independence. He was an educated white and part of the Méridan elite, and since he had nothing to do with the Mayan struggle, the name didn't offend them. In this way the Yucatán Peninsula, was divided into three almost equal portions: Yucatán, Campeche, and Quintana Roo.

Don Andrés Quintana Roo

Quintana Roo

In the early years of the 20th century, there were more uprisings and conspiracies in Yucatán, but they were all effectively suppressed. The government tried to colonize the new territory of Quintana Roo and build infrastructure, but the Mayans rose up again in 1907 and 1912.

Eventually, with the triumph of the 1910 Revolution in Mexico, an eminently social and peasant movement, things began to change. The Yucatecan landowners increased their laborers' salary, granted them Sunday rest, had the hacienda stores sell at the same price as in the free market, and reduced the number of places where intoxicating beverages were sold. In 1914, while Francisco Villa and Emiliano Zapata advanced on Mexico City and took possession of the National Palace, the governor of Yucatán decreed that the debts of the peasants were extinguished forever and future loans would not be paid with personal work.

The final liberation of the indigenous people would be the work of General Salvador Alvarado, one of the enlightened men of the Mexican Revolution who had studied the socialism and feminist ideas at the beginning of the 20th century. His first action upon arriving in Mérida was to release more than 500 prisoners of war who were humble day laborers. He gave them provisions, money, and train tickets, and he told them to return to their homes in peace because the Revolution would not oppress the unfortunate. As governor, always living a simple and respectful life of provincial customs, he prohibited the forced confinement of workers and the retention of their children. He wrote in his memoirs, "I found Yucatan in full servitude. The powerful lived outside the law, those who, century after century, wanted the unfortunate outcast who rose from the ground to tremulously kiss their hand, as in a ceremony of feudal vassalage, the servant with his back open by the whip of the foremen, thus making the degradation of the human species an almost sacred ritual. Also outside the law lived the landowner who owned the Indian, exactly like a cow, wounded with his mark."

Alvarado

Governor Alvarado established laws to protect working women and children, and he declared the work of the housemaids to be free, forcing the masters to compensate them when they seduced them. He explained, "Just as there were thousands of slaves in the fields, there were also thousands of poor women in the cities subjected to domestic servitude in a way that, with a mask of paternality, was in fact positive slavery. The service of the rich and well-off houses was performed by dozens of poor women, Indian or mestizo, who lived locked up, working incessantly, with no more salary than the roof, clothes and food; useless for the free life, sterile for love, dead for hope. And the Revolution by my hand, opened the doors of their prisons, let them know that they were free and that they had the right to live."

Finally, Alvarado ordered the masters to pay the servants with a salary, not in kind. In conjunction with those measures, he closed bars, brothels, and churches, while establishing more than 1,000 schools.

Once Yucatán was pacified, General Alvarado went to Santa Cruz de Bravo, where the Maya were still fighting, and demanded that the authorities withdraw and give them back their lands. Alvarado handed them the town and surrounding lands. The natives took the territory, but, distrustful for centuries, they went ahead and destroyed the railroad tracks and the telephone and telegraph lines, along with everything else previously built by the government. Chief Francisco May assumed command as head of a kind of military theocracy, and shortly after that he got President Venustiano Carranza to give him the rank of general. The Maya also received a concession to exploit 200,000 hectares of forest tax free, and they were given the ability to operate the railroad, which they thus rebuilt. The global gum boom produced better incomes for the inhabitants, the average worker's hut became a brick house, and the farms passed from having a single pig to a few animals. Along with growing prosperity, the Maya's hatred of whites was diminished.

The Rediscovery of Yucatán

"At four o'clock we left Piste, and very soon we saw rising high above the plain the Castillo of Chichen. In half an hour we were among the ruins of this ancient city, with all the great buildings in full view, casting prodigious shadows over the plain, and presenting a spectacle which, even after all that we had seen, once more excited in us emotions of wonder." - John Lloyd Stephens, *Incidents of Travel in Yucatan* (1843)

The Caste War left a legacy of violence, tensions, and political change, and it was the most expensive conflict in Mexico's history so far, at least in terms of human lives.[7] More than 300,000 people died during the fighting, nearly half of the peninsula's entire population.

If there was any silver lining, it was that the end of the Caste War brought a greater interest in classical Mayan culture, as well as the professionalization of the studies of its monuments and great buildings that had remained under a layer of foliage. Scientific and government institutions participated in several expeditions to unearth the past across the peninsula, as opposed to the so-called era of the explorers who throughout the 19th century had traversed the old territories of

---

[7] The Mexican Revolution (1910-1920) cost a million lives but was nationwide.

the Mayan Empire on their own, taking photographs and drawing pictures of impressive ruins.

The city of Chichen Itza, the Maya's most famous city, came to the world's attention when an American explorer named John Lloyd Stephens published *Incidents of Travel in Yucatan*, with illustrations of the city and its surroundings. His work had such an impact that from then on, and throughout the next century, Yucatán would be visited by dozens of explorers, travelers and expeditions. Driven by scientific spirit, and thinking of the Mayans not only as a people to exploit, the expeditions would reveal the degree of progress that the Mayan Empire had reached in the classical era.

Stephens

Another explorer, Teobert Maler, visited the peninsula at the end of the 19th century with a few Mayans, who cleared the buildings covered with vegetation and allowed him to photograph the hidden facades. Sylvanus G. Morley arrived in Mexico in 1907, visited Chichen Itza, and learned about the explorations that the American consul was carrying out on the site. There he had the opportunity to observe the dredging of the sacred cenote of Chichen Itza, and he saw the workers dig up archeological objects thrown in by the natives to protect them from the evangelizers.

Beginning in 1924, the Carnegie Institution of Washington, D.C. reconstructed several buildings at Chichen Itza, notably the Temple of the Warriors and El Caracol, the Maya astronomical observatory. At the same time, the Mexican government restored El Castillo, the great pyramid, and the Great Ball Court.

The discovery of the tomb of Pacal I by Alberto Ruz Lhuillier had a significant impact on Mayan archeology since this finding confirmed that both the Maya and the Egyptians built funerary monuments for their rulers, and that they had complex cosmogonic concepts related to death and beyond. Thereafter, the archaeological finds multiplied.

In terms of the modern era, one of the greatest developments in the history of the Yucatán Peninsula was the construction of Cancun, in the state of Quintana Roo (formerly Chan Santa Cruz). One of the most visited tourist places in Mexico today, Cancun, a city that emerged from the jungle, was made possible thanks to its crystalline waters with goldfish, white sands, and the proximity of archaeological ruins that arouse the interest of tourists who are otherwise accustomed to colder climates. To many, Cancun is more like a paradise.

Cancun was a fishing village in 1970 when investment from the Mexican government started to flow with the support of the International Development Bank (IDB). The population of Cancun went from 88,000 people in 1971, with the majority still dedicated to agriculture, to more than a million people today. Despite being a tiny area compared to the rest of Mexico, Cancun receives a third of the investment in tourism at the national level. It currently has more than 100,000 hotel rooms, the same number as New York City, and its airport is the second busiest in the country after Mexico City's. The millions of tourists who visit its beaches usually pay a visit to Chichen Itza, a couple of hours away by car.

Along with Chiapas, the state of Yucatán is home to the largest indigenous population in the country, and the natives still make up about 40% of its inhabitants. The Mayan language is still spoken by many people, and the cult of the Talking Cross has continued. In many towns, especially in the east of the peninsula, it is still possible to find families that live "in *solares* (large family compounds), surrounded by fruit trees, farm animals, and various outbuildings. The men cultivate corn, beans, squash, and other staples in nearby milpas, while women dressed in impeccably clean huipiles prepared tortillas and tended to children and household animals." The region, however, is gradually being affected by tourist expansion, and, as in every major cosmopolitan city, Cancun has suffered the plague of organized crime.

Unlike other Native American groups, the Maya managed to survive its encounters with colonizers over the last 500 years. They have managed to retain a strong sense of independence, and though they struggled with diseases, repression, and then the absorption and destruction of many expressions of their culture, they resisted assimilation. They had to make many concessions to survive in a country where, since the beginning of the Spanish Conquest, they were at a clear social and political disadvantage. The rebellions of Canek in the colonial era and the Caste War in the 19th century are just a few examples of resistance and struggle.

Thanks to the vigor of their historical traditions and culture, several Mayan communities continue to survive in Mexico and Central America, speak their languages, and perpetuate ideas and customs of their own. Anthropologist Victor Montejo, a Jakaltec Maya from Guatemala, has written eloquently about the tenacity of Maya culture: "Mayas have faced much adversity throughout almost five hundred years of Western domination. They have met these extreme hardships with effective strategies of cultural survival. Each ethnic group has managed to save, transform, and continue different aspects of that ancient Maya culture that give all modern Maya people their common identity."

Thus, despite its cruelty and destruction, the Caste War may have contributed not only to the resistance and dignification of the native peoples of Yucatán, but also the projection of the Mayan culture and its historic struggle. As a result, the Maya remain respected and appreciated, not only in the Americas, but also across the rest of the world.

Online Resources

Other titles about Mexico by Charles River Editors

Other titles about the Maya on Amazon

Bibliography

Salvador Alvarado. *Actuación Revolucionaria del General Salvador Alvarado en Yucatán,* 1955.

Eric N. Baklanoff, *Yucatan in an era of globalization*, The University of Alabama Press, 2008.

Alfredo Barrera Rubio. *En busca de los antiguos mayas. Historia de la arqueología de Yucatán*, Dante, 2015.

Diego de Landa, *Relación de las cosas de Yucatán.*

Robert W. Patch. "La rebelión de Jacinto Canek en Yucatán: una nueva interpretación". *Desacatos Revista de Antropología Social*, num. 13, Conacyt, 2003.

Sergio Quezada, *La colonización de los mayas peninsulares*. Gobierno del Estado de Yucatán, 2011.

Nelson Reed, *La guerra de castas en Yucatán*, Ediciones Era, 2007.

Douglas W. Richmond, *Conflict and Carnage in Yucatán: Liberals, the Second Empire and Maya Revolutionaries, 1855–1876*. University of Alabama Press, 2015.

John Kenneth Turner, *Barbarous Mexico*, University of Texas Press, 1976.

Free Books by Charles River Editors

We have brand new titles available for free most days of the week. To see which of our titles are currently free, click on this link.

Discounted Books by Charles River Editors

We have titles at a discount price of just 99 cents everyday. To see which of our titles are currently 99 cents, click on this link.